Step-Up Your Business!

Boost Your Sales in a Matter of Days

By: Laura McKinley

9781635014402

PUBLISHERS NOTES

Disclaimer – Speedy Publishing LLC

This book was originally printed before 2014. This is an adapted reprint by Speedy Publishing LLC with newly updated content designed to help readers with much more accurate and timely information and data.

Speedy Publishing LLC

40 E Main Street, Newark, Delaware, 19711

Contact Us: 1-888-248-4521

Website: http://www.speedypublishing.co

REPRINTED Paperback Edition: 9781635014402:

Manufactured in the United States of America

DEDICATION

This book is dedicated to Gerald. Thank you for the love and support.

TABLE OF CONTENTS

CHAPTER 1- THE SMALLEST THINGS MAKE THE MOST IMPACT

Did you know that there are many little things that you can do to your website, blog, sales letter or product that can drastically affect the size of your PayPal account?

You see, there are a zillion and one products available on the Internet – and so is the Internet population! Making money online is all about the numbers. Because an Internet marketer can have hundreds to thousands of visitors visiting his website every day, even the smallest changes can increase their profits dramatically.

Just take a look at the math.

A small tweak in a marketer's email headline will cause an additional 2% to open the E-mail (Let's assume the list size is about

50,000). If his 'open rate' used to be about 10%, an additional 2% would get at least an extra 1,000 pairs of new eyeballs reading your E-mail!

But that is just the E-mail marketing aspect. What we want to do is to make our website convert like crazy! Imagine if among that additional 1,000 people, you are able to sell at least a thousand extra dollars' worth of E-products to them by making minor tweaks to your website?

Imagine... if you are doing this OVER AND OVER AGAIN?

Make no mistake about it.

There are many things we as marketers can do in order to enhance our business and increase our profits. If we aren't doing everything we possibly can to make the most out of our businesses, then we are leaving money on the table, right? It's not rocket science and it certainly isn't difficult to understand.

This report is going to discuss 10 important, and possible crucial facts/ideas that if implemented, will increase your business as well as your profits.

Here they are:

There are many things we as marketers can do in order to enhance our business and increase our profits. If we aren't doing everything we possibly can to make the most out of our businesses, then we are leaving money on the table, right? It's not rocket science and it certainly isn't difficult to understand.

Laura McKinley
Here they are:

1. Prioritize

The first tip for enhancing your business and increasing your profits in 2009 that I would like to share with you is that you must 'prioritize' when you are working or conducting your business. This can be done in a lot of ways and in a lot of different aspects.

For instance, what is a bigger priority, hanging out on the Warrior Forum's Main Discussion section, OR writing an article (or two or three!) to promote your website, product or services? Obviously the latter should be a higher priority, but which one do you often choose to do instead? An article can be written in anywhere from 15 minutes, to an hour. Even I find myself spending anywhere from 10 minutes to several hours on the forum when I could be doing much more for my business. (Not that the information on the forum doesn't help your business, because it very much does!).

This is just one example of something you can do to prioritize your TIME better. You can also prioritize other things just as strategically. You can prioritize which projects or tasks you will work on first and in order of importance.

One problem that many marketers (and Warriors) face is checking their stats or email much more often than needed, which takes them away from important tasks that should be getting done.

2. Go Offline

This is a method that I myself have only recently gotten involved in. You would be surprised at how well this actually works, for MANY online niches. The ones that work best are:

Step-up Your Business!
- Make Money Online Opportunities

- Work from Home

- Weight Loss

- Travel

- Health/Fitness

- Beauty

There are quite a number of ways you can market your online business, offline. A very basic way is to have business cards made with your website address (URL) on the card nice and big. Leaving these business cards in the appropriate places (provided you have permission) works wonders!

For example, if you have a website that is in the 'make money online' niche, the best places to leave your business cards would be next to things that have to do with money. Next to the scratch-off lottery tickets at a convenient store or gas station is an excellent place to put a stack of cards that says "Make Money Online, Work From Home" or something related and more specific, such as "Earn $500 from Home!" and of course have your website URL nice and bold.

This can generate a lot of website traffic that you may have NEVER got if you hadn't put business cards in these key places. The weight loss niche is also a hot one. You can leave business cards at ice cream shops, burger places, gyms, spas, gas stations, convenient stores, etc. and get a great response as well.

Aside from business cards, you can use Flyers, Car Magnets, Signs, Newspaper Ads, Television or Radio Ads (can get a little expensive, but can also produce excellent results). Getting a local radio station to mention your URL and a brief description or sales pitch for your site can get you a lot of business and be very much worth a couple thousand dollars.

You can get as creative as you want with offline promotions. You can do direct mailing, put little signs in the ground where there is a lot of traffic (similar to the campaigning signs you see around everywhere only advertising your site). It is important that you do not break any city, county or federal rules and laws in your marketing efforts so always do your research as to what is allowed and what isn't.

3. Learn a New Skill

By learning a new skill (that there is a demand for of course), there is no way that you will not increase your profits in the coming months and years. Personally, I think that copywriting is the best skill you could possibly learn, or at very least brush up on. If you can write effective sales copy, not only can you make a lot of money by writing the sales letters to promote your own products or affiliate promotions, but you can also charge an arm and a leg for your sales copywriting services.

If copywriting is to time consuming of a venture for you to get into, or you are not interested in it at all, there are many skills you can learn that can make you money right on the Warrior Forum itself, or on other Freelance websites as well as offline -- such as:

- Web design

- Article writing

Step-up Your Business!
- Graphic design

- SEO Techniques

- LSI Techniques

- Learn some Time Management skills

- .PHP, MySQL, HTML, Java, Flash, Ruby on Rails, or any of these related skills are highly sought after and pay very well

- How to create your own product

- How to land a JV

- And again, anything creative that you can come up with!

Whether you learn the new skill to use solely in your own advertising campaigns or so that you can sell your services -- you will profit highly from acquiring one of these skills. If you learn the skill to use for yourself, you will save a ton of money on outsourcing; therefore your profits will have increased. In the same way, if you learn the skill in order to sell your services you will also (obviously) profit greatly from that route.

Take article writing for example. If you learn how to do this simple skill, you can profit in at least 3 ways that I can think of off the top of my head:

1. Writing articles for yourself to promote your products/services, etc.

2. Saving money by not having to outsource

3. Selling your article writing services for even more profit

You will leave money on the table again if you don't learn a new skill this year. How many times do we leave money on the table on a daily basis? Think about it. All these extra nooks and crannies that we can squeeze profits and long term income streams out of can really add up to a lot, and make a significant difference in the success of one's business.

CHAPTER 2- PROCESSES AND CHANGES THAT HAVE LONG-TERM EFFECTS ON YOUR BUSINESS

- **Add a New Marketing Technique to Your Routine**

This tip is an extremely effective one. Let's say you have 4 main marketing methods that you use to promote your business. Just as an example, let's say those 4 methods were:

- 1. Pay-Per-Click Advertising (PPC)

- 2. Classified Ads (Craigslist, etc.)

- 3. Social Network Marketing

- 4. Blogging

This is an excellent group of advertising methods to combine and implement.

Laura McKinley

But, what if you were to add another marketing method in there, such as article writing for example, then that would make it 5 methods instead of 4, making your new 'article marketing' method encompass a whopping 20% of your advertising!

That means you can add a lot of business and increase your profits by a significant amount by adding new marketing methods to your existing campaign.

You can add more than one method for even better results. There are many marketing techniques that are great to add to your repertoire, like:

• SEO

• Link Building

• Article Writing

• PPC

• Blogging

• Social Network Marketing

• Classified Ad Marketing

• Offline Marketing (Business Cards, Flyers, Car Magnet, etc.)

• Offline Newspaper Classified Ads

• Answer Board Marketing

• Video Marketing (YouTube Marketing, etc.)

Step-up Your Business!

- Building a List

- Landing a JV

- Email Marketing

- Forum Marketing (Other than IM Niche)

- Outsourcing

- Etc.

There are more, but I am sure there is at least ONE of the above things that you are not doing at all, or not doing enough of.

If you add one or more of the above marketing methods to your existing marketing efforts, I guarantee you will increase your profits and enhance your business over this next upcoming year.

- **Outsource**

Every successful person and/or corporation is involved in outsourcing of some sort. Usually, this is the very key that allows them to achieve the level of success that they do. If the owner of the Ford Motor Company had to make all the cars himself, do you think the company would be where they are today? The fact that they can outsource their work to enough people, who know what they are doing, makes them able to reach the success level that they desire.

You've heard the term, "Two heads are better than one." This rings true in a lot of aspects of life. It's kind of like that will outsourcing. If you can write 5 articles a day, that is great. However, if you can write 5 a day, and outsource another 5 articles per day, then that makes it 10 articles a day, instead of 5.

That just DOUBLED your marketing efforts right there, so as I said in the title of this report...You will increase your profits and enhance your business if you implement these tips. If you DOUBLE your output, you will have DOUBLE the results. Imagine if you outsourced a lot more often, or on a broader scale. Also, outsourcing will allow you to use the millionaire mindset of knowing that there are people out there who can do a better job than you can when it comes to certain tasks or skills. So instead of competing against these people, hire them!

Think about it, if you outsource a sales letter to a TOP sales copywriter, chances are that your product offer will convert A LOT more than it would if you wrote your own sales copy, or looked for a really low bargain. With excellent copywriting, an offer will tend to convert much better and sell many more copies -- which again, enhance your business as well as increase your profits.

- **Do Video Marketing**

If you have not yet gotten into video marketing yet, this is SERIOUSLY the time to do so. Again, this is something else that can also be outsourced or done quite easily by you, at home. YouTube.com is owned by Google and everybody knows how fast your video gets indexed by Google for a specific keyword(s), and the traffic that a single video can generate.

If you are thinking that there is NO way that you can get involved in video marketing, because you just don't have the skills, equipment, or money -- Baloney!

Step-up Your Business!

If you've ever filmed a friend or family member with a digital video camera or one of those camcorders from the 1980s, you can be a video marketer.

Basically, you can use a simple digital camera that has video capabilities, or you can borrow one from a friend (I am sure someone you know has one!). You can even ask them to help film you and get them in on it.

All you have to do is talk for a few minutes about whatever niche market you are in. You can give away tips, advice, or give a product review for a product that you are promoting. It can be either a product or service that you created, or one that you are promoting as an affiliate of course.

Putting the KEYWORD that you are targeting in the TITLE of the video is the best way to get your video listed on the search engines (Google) the fastest and highest ranking. There are also keyword tags that you can input in the 'tags' section of your video. It is very easy to get a FREE account with YouTube.com and it is also very easy and FREE to post as many videos as you like! This is a very powerful marketing tool right at your fingertips, and it's free.

Additionally, once you post a video to YouTube, not only will you receive traffic to your video from YouTube surfers, but also from Google searchers...But you will also be able to place the video in your website. They give you the embedded HTML code for you to simply 'copy and paste' into your website and/or blog. This gives your website the power of video -- without costing you a dime! You are surely leaving money on the table if you do not get involved with video marketing over this next year.

This tip has served as yet another way to enhance your Business and increase your Profits in the coming year(s).

• Add a New Niche

There is more than likely a niche that you have not yet gotten into or have been wanting to get into for a while, but are procrastinating out of fear of failure, or any reason for that matter.

Well, I guarantee that you are not involved in every single profitable niche. So, the question arises, "Why not add another profit stream to your business if you can?"

I personally can't think of a reason why not to, can you?

Let's say you are in the IM niche and the Weight Loss niche. You may be leaving money on the table by not getting into another hot niche right now, such as holiday gifts, or a completely new niche that will be a permanent income stream, like Acne or Fitness.

Breaking into a new niche can be easy, or it can be difficult depending on how YOU make it. Getting into the acne niche (just as an example), can be as easy as putting up a site or blog about acne. Write several articles or product reviews about acne and acne products. If you cannot do the research and write articles yourself, you can again, outsource them for as low as $4 an article for good quality articles. You can then place Google AdSense ads on your site as well as affiliate links to products that are of good quality, deliver what they promise, convert well and pay good commissions. 60-75% is the norm nowadays for most eBooks and software that are sold through marketplaces like Clickbank.com.

Once you have a site/blog set up with articles/reviews, AdSense and affiliate links, you are good to go! You can promote your new niche site via PPC, or you can write articles (or have them outsourced again) and submit them to EzineArticles.com or any other major article directory. It's anywhere from 5-10 hours' worth of work to get it going, and it can cost you little to nothing and you will have a new revenue stream that will potentially bring in long term revenue.

This tip will also surely enhance your business and increase your profits in the coming year(s), provided you take action and implement it fully.

So what if you fail? That is what business and being successful is all about, trial and error. Successes and failures, there is no such thing as a perfect world. And most of the time if you pick a good niche follow your goals and stay focused you will succeed.

• **Take the Time to Prospect**

You cannot achieve more success, earn more money or anything of the sort if you don't seek out the opportunities and then grab them! There is a ton of prospecting for you to do from now and until you retire. Prospecting can come in many forms, you can do it small scale and seek out clients locally and on places like the Warrior Forum, who need services or products that you can offer them. Or, it can be done on a larger scale where you look to land some JV's (Joint Ventures) or invest in a business, find new niches, etc.

Prospecting can land you one extra deal this year, or it can land you 1,000 extra deals! How's that for increasing your profits? Even if you successfully obtain one client or make only one sale as a direct result of your extra 'prospecting' you will enhance your business and increase your profits.

Go out there and see what's hot -- and what people want. It's very easy to stick with what you already know and are routinely doing on a daily or weekly basis. But, if you take the time to prospect a little bit, and pretend like it is the beginning of your online career again and you are super enthusiastic about all the fresh opportunities and money making ideas that are surrounding you. You will surely find a thing (or two) that will lead to a long term income and profit stream.

Remember, we're beefing up your business here, I am not saying to do these types of things all the time. But once every year or couple years is a good time to update, upgrade and take your business to the next level, no matter how small or large your business is.

Prospect for new clientele, prospect for new business ideas -- Prospect.

- **It's the Double Effect!**

This is something I like to call the 'Double Effect' and it is a theory/technique/strategy that I use to enhance my business and increase my profits every couple years.

The Double Effect can be applied to many different circumstances, for instance, let's talk about it on a smaller scale for a moment. If you write articles to promote your website and it is working very well for you, what could you do to double that success? Simple. Outsource the exact number of articles that you write, so if you write 5 articles, outsource 5 articles and now you'll have 10 articles. This will mean that your efforts, as well as your traffic, as well as your PROFITS, will double.

Okay, so even if they don't double per se, what if they improved by 150%? That would still be MORE profit in your pocket at the end of the day. You don't even have to outsource or pay money to get double the work done sometimes. You can write the whole 10 yourself instead of just writing 5, or you can have a friend, family member or significant other help write for you as well, provided you give them a little bit of training.

What else could you do in your online business world that could DOUBLE your profits?

• Can you come out with two videos instead of just one?

• Can you market to 2 niches instead of one?

• Can you charge double for one of your products or services instead of possibly selling yourself short?

• Can you possibly (with the help of some outsourcing) pull off two launches instead of one this year?

• Can you put up a website AND a blog instead of just one or the other?

• Could you possibly double your PPC Advertising budget, or raise it by any %?

Any of the above tactics would either double your profits or increase them significantly, so there is no reason to ignore the magical potential of the 'Double Effect.'

I personally have my fiancée help me write articles. If I were to write only 5 or 10 a day myself, I would be at a certain level. But since she also writes that many each day, my efforts are doubled, my traffic is doubled, my response is doubled and therefore...my PROFIT is doubled.

Again, it isn't rocket science, but it works and it is a perspective that you should try to embrace.

What if you took it even further and made a 'TRIPLE EFFECT'? That would take a little bit more outsourcing, or tripling the amount of hours you work to accomplish, but triple the income doesn't sound bad to me. Most people don't DO that much work online, so doubling their efforts or even tripling their efforts wouldn't really be that difficult to do. For a more advanced marketer, maybe doubling a few things here and there such as the amount of articles submitted per month or the doubling the price of a product -- while adding a bonus to compensate of course.

- **Follow the Trend**

It is 2008 and drawing closer and closer to 2009. We were supposed to have flying cars by now, but instead we have iPods and eBooks. Well, it's pretty advanced compared to even 15-20 years ago, heck even 10 years ago! A lot of internet marketers stick to what has made them money 'in the past' or they follow a business model that worked for somebody else, 'in the past.' What matters is right now. If a new product comes out tomorrow that sweeps the nation and everybody MUST have one -- your job as a marketer is to go out there and market it! Why would you stay back and market beepers or pagers, when iPhones and BlackBerry phones are the latest and greatest?

When Craigslist was the hottest thing around, I wrote a report about how to advertise effectively and ethically on Craigslist. It sold like hot cakes, because the topic was hot. Most of the time, Amazon.com and eBay.com will be selling the latest and hottest products on the market and therefore you can get a piece of the action by promoting these items as an affiliate. Even the greats have to 'Get with the times' every now and then. Listen to great music artists like Paul McCartney. His hits always fit in with the style of the current time. In the 60's he was writing "She Loves You, Yeah, Yeah, Yeah!" and in the 80's he was writing "Silly Love Songs"

Step-up Your Business!
and "Ebony and Ivory" which are very much 80's style music. Getting with the times is an essential part of your business -- online or off -- and it will most certainly result in your business enhancing and your profits increasing.

Here are some things you can do to follow the trend as far as your internet business is concerned:

- Get into video marketing

- Use Web 2.0 techniques

- Make your site look modern!

- Be involved in social networks (twitter, etc.)

- Have video on your site, as well as new looking Web 2.0 graphics

- Sell Products that are popular NOW, in the current time (day, week, and month)

- Follow the latest rule changes so you can keep up with effective SEO techniques (A lot of people use very outdated SEO tactics that don't work anymore).

- Use LSI Techniques when doing SEO for your site or when writing optimized articles, etc.

- Build a list of opt-in subscribers using a squeeze page

- And anything else that is new, groundbreaking, effective, creative and profitable!

CHAPTER 3- BEING TOO MODEST WON'T GET YOU ANYWHERE!

You can't afford to be too modest when you are trying to market your products on the Internet. Your product and your website on the Internet are like a small drop in a very large ocean. People's attention span is divided amongst millions of websites on the Internet screaming for their attention.

Take for example, the resell rights industry. Online, everyone is selling the same products all over the net. Some price those normally while others sell the products for what someone would pay for a bag of peanuts.

It really seem as though every Tom, Dick and Harry are all resellers online. So what makes you different from the others?

If you want to skyrocket your online profits, you MUST be a branded product!

Step-up Your Business!

You see, the online world is slightly different compared to the real world. Some people might be afraid to blow their horn in public (or to tell others how much money they are making online). But online, you can write (almost) whatever you want on your sales copy or your profile page.

The most important thing you must do is you must stand out from the rest of the crowd!

If you've achieved success in sales, make sure you 'flaunt' your PayPal screen shots before others. Do whatever it takes to let others know what's so good about you. Let them know that you are different. If you do things that are extraordinary, chances are, people will take notice and spread the word.

Laser Targeted Focus

One of the things you must remember about branding is that you must let others out there know what you specialize in.

Take for example – Internet marketing blogs. If you search throughout the blogosphere, you will see a hundreds of blogs out there titled Internet marketing with _____ or _____'s blog on making money online.

There are too many blogs with the theme make money online or Internet marketing so the best way to stand out from the rest is to focus on a particular niche.

Let's say you are an expert at network marketing and you want to market your products online. Even network marketing is so competitive and broad that you have to go 'sub-niche'.

Laura McKinley

You can let others know that in the network marketing world, you are the guy who turns words into profitable copy that attracts downlines like a vacuum cleaner.

You can probably call yourself the networking copy king! (I know this might sound a bit corny, but it sure got your attention now, didn't it?)

If you are in to SEO and you are good at long-tail niches, you should let others know about it rather than just focus on a generic SEO branding. It is easier to go for a sub-niche rather than a generic niche.

Use your imagination and brand yourself creatively!

Testimonial Placement

Few would believe you if you say it yourself, but by getting a testimonial from a well-respected marketer in the niche you are in, you can be sure to increase your credibility.

Don't grab any testimonial from just ANY guy or girl. Make sure you let the expert who is providing the testimonial to review you or the product (or you can do some work for them in exchange for a testimonial).

By placing the best and most relevant testimonials at the right place in your sales copy, you can be sure to increase your business profits easily.

CHAPTER 4- STRIVE FOR CUSTOMERS TO RECOGNIZE YOUR BRAND ALMOST IMMEDIATELY

Branding is all about image of a business. The concept doesn't only include style, emblems and logos but also the image of quality perceived. The image perceived may be of total quality, reliability, and more.

Branding is about the business and how a business is different from the competitors. The purpose of a brand is to distinguish yourself from your competitors. Once you make a distinguishing impact then an advertising campaign can be much more effective.

Laura McKinley

The success of a company can be determined by a brand. Branding includes many factors which help a company become successful. These factors may include a website, marketing efforts, and anything that gives a company an identity. Consumers trust wholeheartedly a corporate image because there is a psychology in motivating the purchasing decisions.

All companies should practice branding. Brick and mortar business and online companies benefit through branding methods. It is common for smaller companies and online businesses to fail due to a lack of understanding about the importance and factors of a good brand.

Branding ensures professionalism with a company. It seals the deal on an entire package. A small company with a brand looks just as good as a large corporation when they practice the right techniques. Brands enhance your confidence as a business owner but also in the consumers that you really can deliver what you promise.

Branding offers consistency with a business. It gives direction to employees and customers know what to expect. Consistency can be performed through the use of things like business cards, t-shirts, and more. Consistency includes visibility techniques that are professional and will remain in the memory of a consumer.

One concept that consumers often attach to a brand is called brand equity. A brand is often considered to be an asset also. For example, if you have developed a very good brand that is well known as being a top distributor of massage chairs and you have a competitor with a brand known to provide defective products, your brand will be worth more.

Step-up Your Business!
The Basics of Branding You Ought to Master

Branding is all about what the customers perceive of your company. Your brand is the promise that you intend to make to the customers. The ultimate goal is to spark an emotional connection in order to create a positive feeling resulting of loyalty to a specific product from the customers.

Most customers hold true to products they enjoy. It is very common for a customer to be impressed with a brand and continue to buy a product based on that brand. You want to create these feelings of loyalty to bring the customers back for more. This is the ultimate goal.

Mission and Vision of Your Company

The mission and vision of your company should uphold excellence in providing a quality product to customers that you care about. These are statements about your company regarding the ultimate goals you wish to achieve with in your endeavors. Many companies focus their vision or mission on their employees while others extend their mission outward to the customers. There should be a fine mix here with both.

Many customers do not read into a vision or mission statement too often. However, that doesn't mean that you shouldn't take it seriously. Your vision and mission are both a part of the branding process because they define what your company is all about. These two statements need to be believed and practiced by employees and all staff of the company.

Benefits and Features of Your Products or Services

A big part of creating a brand for your business is proving to the customers why your products and services are the best to buy. Differentiation takes place here but you need to prove the benefits to the consumers. Determine what the benefits are with the products you offer, the services you offer, or something else. Why does the customer benefit when they shop or buy from you? You will have a very hard time establishing a brand if you cannot determine the benefits or your products or services.

The features of your products and services are also important and they go hand in hand with the benefits. The features of a specific product should provide a benefit. Determine the features and the ones that stand out from the rest or provide the biggest benefit may be a target for the marketing campaign.

Customers Perception Today

Branding is about customer's perception. When you want to create a brand you want to create a perception of the customer that you are the best, provide quality, or maybe even more.

It is important to have a good idea of what the customers currently think of you when you are building a branding campaign. Today customers may not know that you exist or they may have a negative feel for your business because you haven't been practicing proper methods. Have a clear understanding on exactly what the customers think of you.

If you are unsure what the customers think of you then you may need to send out surveys and questionnaires. These types of things can help you get a good idea where you stand with the perception of the customers. It is okay if it is bad today. It will give you something to build on with your branding campaign.

Qualities Perceived by the Customers

The next thing you need to do with a branding campaign is to determine the different qualities that are perceived about your products by the customers. Do you have a good reputation with the consumer world for providing total quality in your products or are your products considered to be garbage and not worth the money?

The qualities of your business may be many things. When you think about how customers consider the qualities of your business, make sure you consider the products you offer, the customer support you provide, your image, or anything else that would make a customer think of quality coming from your company.

The vision and mission statement are very important for every business no matter how big or small. Make sure that your brand works well and matches what you say you want to deliver. Determine what the benefits and features of your business are and have a clear picture on this. You will need this information to provide a clear picture when you focus on developing your brand.

Also learn about what the customers really think of you. You might think customers absolutely love you when they are really bashing you on the quality of your product. Knowing what the customers think is very important. Creating a brand based on customer input can be successful, especially if you change the design of something for the customers. This gives them a sense of ownership and it shows them you really do care.

So, Who Are Your Audience?

Audience is everything. If you do not know the audience that you are targeting then you cannot begin creating a brand for a product or a company. There are many reasons that audience must be considered. Knowing your audience well will work for you in the long run.

The audience is the targeted customer base that you are hoping to reach out to for purchasing your product. Audience may include gender, age, geographical regions, and more.

The age of an audience must be considered when branding occurs. This is because if you are targeting a younger and more hip crowd they may want to see a brand that is vibrant and more hip. If your audience is older and more sophisticated then they may be looking for a brand displaying more professionalism.

Gender of an audience is often an issue if you are selling women's clothing, men's hats, or other items. However, when you create a brand for a man, remember that you can create ad campaigns targeting the women to purchase the products as gifts for men.

Income isn't something that many people think about when they consider an audience when developing a brand. This is often where companies go wrong. If you are selling a video gaming system that is several hundreds of dollars in a local store down the street and the average income of families in the area is less than $25,000 a year they may not be able to afford the product. You cannot sell an expensive product to a poor audience. Also, people with a very high income may not consider purchasing a very cheap product. The value of your brand must match the income of the people you think will be your primary target as customers.

Step-up Your Business!

Geographical regions are also very important. Many people open businesses and try to sell products and services where there just isn't a need. This is a good way to fail. For example, if you have a company selling snow shovels then it wouldn't make sense to try to sell them to home owners in Florida. Know your geographical locations and which regions will benefit the most from your product or services.

Know Your Audience

There are many things about your audience that you must know when you are creating a brand. If you do not have a clear understanding of which your audience is then you will fail.

When you determine who your audience is, the next step you need to do is to narrow your choices down based on the age, gender (only if specific), geographical region (only if specific), and income levels, and so on. Your audience will be defined as something like 20-30 year old, male golfers that are left handed.

Some brands may not be this specific. However, the more you can narrow down your audience the more your brand will separate you from the competition. This means you will have less competition to worry about also.

Branding by Your Audience

Branding by your audience will allow you to be more successful with sales and develop long lasting customers that are dedicated to you. Targeting the wrong audience can cause problems with credibility and trust.

Older groups of people often want to see a brand as one they can trust. They want credibility and a professional look. If the image appears to be young or unprofessional then you may find that your revenues are lacking.

The same practice rings true with a younger crowd. If you are targeting a young crowd and your brand is too professional and comes across as boring then kids will not be interested in what you have to offer. For example, if your target audience is to sell super-fast toy cars to five year old boys then you want a very exciting brand that is fun. If your brand is professional and so is your appearance it will be hard to convince a 5 year old that the cars are really fast.

Always brand by audience. Find out what they want to see. You may even want to talk to different age groups and find out what they would like to see. This would be a good place to start.

CHAPTER 5- IT'S OK TO GO CRAZY ON THE GRAPHICS

You see, most of the time, there are many people out there who actually ignore the appearance of their products. They would spend tons of money on their ghostwriters, their website, their autoresponder and even their work force, but the moment they neglect the appearance of their E-cover, they lose many precious sales because their E-cover for their E-book isn't attractive enough.

The truth would scare you – many DO judge a book by its cover.

If you invest in a good action script you can easily enhance the appearance of your E-cover: You can change it from a flat one to a more realistic cover that will convert more visitors into buyers.

Mini-Site Banners

Mini-site banners are equally important as well. Imagine the first thing people see other than the opening headline of the sales copy or landing page is the banner itself.

Don't use just ANY banner

There are tons of PLR books out there that comes with the PSD file for the sales letter.

You can easily make changes in Adobe Photoshop to get the best colors or fonts that you will need without investing too much into graphics design.

Product Pictures

You can also combine pictures together to make the appearance of the full package even more enticing.

Use a Different Color for Your Headline

In a sales copy, the most important aspect of the sales process is in getting the prospect's attention. Therefore, the headline is the most crucial aspect of the entire sales copy.

After all, if the headline doesn't entice readers to read the rest of the sales letter, it is pointless to write the sales letter in the first place!

Step-up Your Business!

You see, by tweaking several aspects of the same headline, you are able to tap in to several psychological aspects of the prospect and get them to take action by starting to read the rest of the sales letter.

Minor changes such as switching between RED and BLACK, using a series of UNDERLINES and highlights, you will be able to bring more life to your headline and increase your chances of scoring another sale.

Use Graphics to Make a Point

Often when people are looking through a sales copy, a lot of them do not read the sales letter line by line.

They often scan through the sales copy and they arrive at the end of the sales copy just to see how much it costs. The use of graphics is one of the most effective ways to reach 'scanners'.

For example: If you are selling a membership site that provides the best content for resellers to market themselves, you can tell them:

"Would you rather catch small fishes with what you are doing now or buy this membership and your business will bring in nothing but big fishes?"

I think the illustrations will bring home the point!

Chapter 6- Are You Ready to Squeeze Out Sales From Your Market Niche?

Maximizing AdSense

Here are some 4 ways to tweak your site and you will be able to make more money from AdSense.

1. Use only one format when you are choosing your AdSense layout. The more consistent your design, the easier it is for people to click on your ads. Your goal is to try to 'mask' the ads to look more like links within the webpage. Sometimes, they may not feel that they are clicking on AdSense but at least it brings in more money.

2. Choose a color that blends with the background of your niche site. Once again, this also improves the clicks on the ads and hence, your income will increase as well.

3. Try and locate your AdSense ads where it is easier for people to see. Don't put them at places where people won't scroll too because that will prevent them from clicking them (or even seeing them for that matter).

4. Go for relevant keywords in your ads. According to some experts, Google doesn't really care about your content – rather, it scans the title, description and the URL.

Affiliate Program Reviews

One of the best ways to promote a product on a niche site is to use a 'review' format.

Take for example – a movie. When someone goes online to read about the review, they will tend to believe the reviewer and keep their opinion in mind when they go to a cinema.

Notice however that the person reading the review will probably believe what the reviewer is saying. They don't sit around wondering if the movie critic is getting affiliate commissions from telling people to watch the movie.

Most of the time, Internet marketers or even niche marketers become too 'sales pitchy' when it comes to affiliate product recommendations. They don't realize that a simple and 'unbiased' review will easily sway a buyer's mind.

Laura McKinley

If you were to talk about a product as though you were reviewing from a 'neutral' point of view, you will be able to get more relevant traffic to your affiliate programs.

You should create titles for your post like – ABC product review, or a review on product XYZ.

After all, people would rather trust a neutral party rather than a salesman.

Chapter 7- Teach People What You Know Through Videos

Did you know that a simple video on YouTube can drastically increase your conversion rates and skyrocket your profits?

Aurelius Tjin of the infamous Copy and Paste Graphics 2 once launched a fire sale on his birthday. What he did was he created a short video teaching people how to use the products in the fire sale.

His affiliates sent their traffic to the video page and immediately, sales started coming in faster than ever.

If you want to convince buyers to invest in your product, creating a video designed to educate prospects will get you more sales than ever. As a matter of fact, creating a video is often much easier for some people (especially for those who hate writing).

Get Them to Take Action

Another well-known marketer made full use of video for building his list. John Reese of the infamous Blog Rush used the power of Viral marketing to make Blog Rush one of the most used widgets in the blogosphere.

How did he do it?

Well, he simply referred people to watch a video on how to drive massive FREE traffic to your blog and he implemented a very simple way for people to sign up and refer their friends.

Their friends watched the same video and they did the same thing until almost every blog on the Internet started using Blog Rush.

He achieved this all because he had a powerful video that made people take action immediately.

CHAPTER 8- OTHER EFFECTIVE METHODS TO BOOST SALES

1.Add complimentary up sells and cross sells on your thank-you/download pages.

When your customer arrives at your download pages after a purchase there's solid evidence to say he or she will still be in a buying mood.

Make sure you have another offer on this page because you can easily pick up additional sales with only the tiniest amount of effort.

For example:

When you add a link to a second offer in an upgrade "welcome" email, you will generate an extra $13147.31 in pure profit on just one web site.

Then by adding in a 2nd cross sell (in Feb 2007) that total was increased by an extra $500 in commissions against a recommended product. Think about it – these secondary promotions offered new members (customers) with a tempting saving – they get a great deal and we add extra profit to our yearly income as a result.

If these stats continue (and there's absolutely no reason why they won't) we'll add $5000-$10000 in extra profit this year to our business.

2.Use bump ups on your order pages

When a customer is ready to buy and they have their credit card in their hand, why not ask them if they'd like to add additional and complimentary products or services at a discount right there and then.

Here's an example:

We started offering "bump ups" on one of our membership sites. For everyone who orders an upgraded membership we simply offer them access to more of our sites with a huge saving to do it as they upgrade.

The key is simplicity – all they are required to do is just click a few boxes on the order form and make the one payment. Everything is then added into their updated membership area.

Step-up Your Business!
Does it work? You betcha! This one tactic alone has added $9,000.00 in additional sales on just one site and in just one month (Feb 2007).

So what would happen when do this across the board? Hmmm...

But even more interesting is the fact that 11.3% of all customers who bought an upgraded membership also ordered the bump up. Assuming these statistics will remain constant throughout the year we just increased our annual income by 11.3%! Most fortune companies would kill to have an 11% annual revenue increase. And you can achieve all that from just a few days of research and work setting up the system.

3.Monetize your login pages.

Now this is something we see absolutely no one doing at the moment. Will you be the next?

We've all seen those blank empty login pages right? You know, put in your username and password and click login – the end. Not very exciting and not making the owner a single cent.

Here's an example:

What is your membership site has 100,000 members and you get an average of 1% to login everyday (including new members and returning members). That's 1,000 visitors every day to your login page. Wouldn't it be cool to offer them something, especially the returning members? Duh, that is a no brainer!

Well, I wanted to test out the theory – so we set that up this year on all our login pages. But we didn't just put one little add on it or a link, we went all out! We have a column listing all our in-house membership sites and products. We have another column listing our JV partner sites (these are reserved for our best JV partners).

We also added a "featured site of the day" too. While we don't sell these spaces, (we certainly could and you could too). We've been offered money for that "real estate" but turned the offers down because it's not for sale.

Results: In just one month we got thousands of additional visitors to our membership sites and our JV partner's sites.

4. Exit/Log-Out pages from your membership site.

Yeah, we all know about exit pages don't we? So how come not everyone uses these properly on their own membership sites? Where do your members go to when they log out of your site?

Our entire log-out pages go somewhere. Usually use a page of limited offers, special discounts and new products. Remember not anyone gets your email these days, and new members joining your site didn't get the offer you sent out last week. Seriously there's no better way to passively show an offer than when someone hits the log out link.

As long as they actually like your site and are loyal to your recommendations this can work like gang busters! While most affiliates who send out promos may see lots of sales that day or for a couple of days those orders usually stop coming in unless you keep sending reminder emails. However, by effectively using log out pages we see a steady stream of sales for everything we choose to promote (even if we only send out 1 email for the week).

5. Have a "Top Picks" or "Recommended Resources" page setup on your site.

Step-up Your Business!
Okay, Okay...we agree that this is nothing new or earth shattering with that advice – but why do so few sites use it (or get it wrong)?

For example:

We have a link to that page in every new member welcome email that goes out in the P.S. area (great for long term passive promotion of that page). We also have it higher up in the navigation menu so members and visitors can get to that page anytime.

We also monitor traffic out, see which products and resources listed are the most popular and then which ones are getting sales. All this without the aid of complex mathematical formula (we simply make the ones that aren't selling inactive after a few weeks and add in new resources to replace them.)

We also change the order/position around regularly to make sure each one is seen and to keep the page looking fresh - All of this is done in from our site CMS admin panel. (We can instantly make changes, add new products etc. and it can be done in less than 15 seconds)

Results: This page alone sent thousands of visitors to those product sales pages – in return that generated tens of thousands of dollars in EXTRA commissions for us over the past couple of years. In Jan. 2007 - I added 6 products which came with instant reseller URLs from our MME2 membership site. In just a 6 week period of doing nothing but having these products listed on that page we sold $637.00 of them. All of that is 100% pure, hassle free profit sent right to our PayPal account. And those results can easily add up to thousands of extra profits every year. If I'd of been a paid customer of MME2 (we build it so I didn't need to buy it again. I'd have already made my membership fee back for just 5 minutes of work.

6.Offer your content in different formats

When we launched our audios back in November 2006 we personally sold a record breaking 500 physical copies (we sold on Data CD-ROM) in just a week.

However, once the initial promotion passed sales slowed down considerably to around 10 or 20 copies a week – Now we're sure that the majority of marketers at that point would be tempted to rest on their laurels and then move on to the next product - We didn't

We truly believe in this product and we wanted to keep on selling it to more and more people so we decided to offer the content in an alternative format - We recently (Feb 2007) re-launched the site as a membership site with streaming audios for people who may not have wanted the CD version or who maybe just didn't see the offer first time round –

That decision brought in an additional 600 paid membership sales in less than 2 weeks. It generated over $22,000 in sales and enabled us to get our strategies, tips and marketing ideas into 600 more pairs of hands... We think that's pretty cool!

ABOUT THE AUTHOR

Laura McKinley is a licensed financial adviser for 15 years. She has helped build small businesses from scratch and even maximize the profits of the market niche of old businesses.

A CEO herself, Laura is among a group of CEOs who gather to meet every month to discuss rising trends and also share experiences to empower one another.